# THE
# TENNESSEE
# WALKING
# HORSE

by Charlotte Wilcox

C A P S T O N E   P R E S S
M A N K A T O

# C A P S T O N E    P R E S S
### 818 North Willow Street • Mankato, MN 56001

Printed in the United States of America.

*Library of Congress Cataloging-in-Publication Data*
Wilcox, Charlotte.
    The Tennessee walking horse/by Charlotte Wilcox
    p. cm.
    Includes bibliographical references (p. 46) and index.
    Summary: Offers information about the breed of horses which is popular for riding and for horse shows and which is as famous for its personality as its gait.
    ISBN 1-56065-365-5
    1. Tennessee walking horse--Juvenile literature. [1. Tennessee walking horse. 2. Horses.] I. Title.
SF293.T4 W55
636.1'3--dc20

                                           95-47770
                                              CIP
                                               AC

Photo credits
Faith A. Uridel: cover, 6-10, 17-25, 31-34, 37-42
Voice Magazine: 12-14
Voice Magazine/David Pruett: 26-28
Voice Magazine/Nancy O. Bold-Fletcher: 36

# Table of Contents

Words in **boldface** type in the text are defined
in the Glossary in the back of this book.

# Quick Facts about the Tennessee Walking Horse

## Description

Height:

Tennessee Walking Horses are 15 to 17 **hands** from the ground to the top of the shoulders. That is 60 to 68 inches (152 to 172 centimeters) tall. Horses are measured in hands. One hand equals four inches (10 centimeters).

Weight:

Walkers weigh 1,000 to 1,200 pounds (450 to 540 kilograms).

Physical features:

Walkers have broad chests, short backs, muscular hindquarters, and long, full tails. Tennessee Walking Horses perform a unique running walk. The horse places its back foot in front of the front hoof print when moving.

Colors:

Walkers come in all colors, but especially **chestnut**, **bay**, **sorrel**, **roan**, brown, black, white, and gray. Many Tennessee Walking Horses have white markings.

## Development

History of breed:   Walkers are the result of crossbreeding Thoroughbreds, Standardbreds, Morgans, and American **Saddlebreds** on Tennessee farms in the 1800s.

Place of origin:   Walkers originated in central Tennessee.

Numbers:   About 300,000 Walkers are registered, with more than 7,500 added every year.

## Life History

Life span:   A well-cared-for Tennessee Walking Horse may live from 20 to 30 years.

## Uses

Tennessee Walking Horses are popular family horses. They are used for pleasure and trail riding. Many are also used for horse shows and other competitions.

# Chapter 1

# A Horse Everyone
# Likes to Ride

People usually want two things when they look for a good riding horse. First, they want a horse with a good temper. A horse that likes people is fun to ride. Second, people want a horse that is comfortable to ride. A horse with a smooth ride is more comfortable than a horse with a rough ride.

Many people say Tennessee Walking Horses have the best tempers of any horse breed. They also provide a smooth ride.

**The Tennessee Walking Horse was first bred in Tennessee.**

**Walking Horses are fun to ride because of their good attitude.**

### Gaits

All horses have four natural **gaits**. They can walk, **trot**, **canter**, and **gallop**. The walk is comfortable, but it is slow. The trot is faster, but it is bumpy. The canter is fast and smooth. The gallop is fastest. But, horses cannot canter or gallop for very long. Both horse and rider get tired.

Some horses are **gaited horses**. They are able to move in ways that other horses cannot. They inherit these special gaits from their parents. There are many different gaited breeds in North and South America. They each have their own special way of moving.

Most horses can only give a smooth ride while walking. Gaited horses can move smoothly at faster speeds.

## The Tennessee Walk

The Tennessee Walking Horse has three special gaits. They are the **flat-foot walk**, the **running walk**, and the **rocking-chair canter**. They offer smooth, comfortable rides at faster speeds.

Walking Horses are fun to ride because of their good attitude. Tennessee Walking Horses are popular with families. People who enjoy trail and pleasure riding like Tennessee Walkers, too.

The Tennessee Walking Horse was first bred in Tennessee. Today, they are raised in the United States, Canada, and other countries.

# Chapter 2

# History of the Walking Horse

Gaited horses were popular in the English and French colonies of North America. Most roads were not smooth enough for travel with a horse and buggy. Almost everyone traveled on horseback.

### Horses in the South

Thousands of pioneers moved into Tennessee after the Revolutionary War (1775-1783). They built farms throughout the South. Horses with smooth gaits were treasured. They

Today, Walking Horses are raised in the United States, Canada, and other countries.

were bred to pass on their smooth gaits to their young.

Tennessee's gaited horse had a smooth running walk. It was first called the Plantation Walking Horse or Turn Row Horse. The breed earned these names because it could turn around in a row of crops without stepping on the plants.

The gaited horses of the South were not bred for speed. Farmers wanted a horse that could travel or hunt all day. They wanted a horse they could hitch up to a plow for fieldwork.

Traveling preachers and country doctors wanted a sturdy horse to travel the rough land. Farmwives needed a gentle horse. Their horses had to carry baskets of eggs without breaking them. They had to be smooth enough not to wake the baby strapped behind the saddle.

## Horses in the North

Things were different in the North. Better roads were built. People could ride in buggies pulled by fast-trotting horses. They no longer needed to ride on horseback. Fast-trotting

**Walking Horses offer comfortable rides at faster speeds.**

horses replaced the gaited breeds. Before long, smooth-gaited horses were bred only in the South.

## The First Known Walking Horse

In 1837, a special horse was born on a farm in Kentucky. The horse was named Bald Stockings. He was the foal of a **Standardbred** and a **Thoroughbred**. Bald Stockings was one of the first horses who could do the running walk.

Bald Stockings and similar horses passed the running walk and other gaits on to their young. They were smooth riding horses. They were muscular and good-looking. They had great personalities. They were known as Tennessee Pacers.

## Horses at War

The Civil War broke out in 1861. Some soldiers traveled on horseback. Union cavalrymen from the North rode fast, sturdy Thoroughbreds, Standardbreds, and **Morgans**. Confederate soldiers from the South had

**Tennessee Walking Horses are a good choice for new riders and children.**

smooth-gaited horses they could ride for miles and miles.

Thousands of horses were killed or injured during the four years of the Civil War. Many more ran away when their riders were injured or killed. Soldiers would take all the horses they could find when they captured an area.

### McMeen's Traveler

McMeen's Traveler was a great Walking Horse **stallion** from central Tennessee. He was captured when the Union army attacked his hometown. The Union soldiers took Traveler and six or eight of his **colts** and **fillies**.

The kidnapping of McMeen's Traveler was a huge loss to the town. One woman decided to rescue him. She rode 20 miles to plead with a Union general to help her find the stallion. She convinced the general that Traveler was too old to be useful to the Union army.

The woman's concern for the horse persuaded the general. He agreed to help her

**After the Civil War, breeders in the South were determined to keep the Walking Horse gaits alive.**

find the stallion. Together they searched for the horse. They found McMeen's Traveler lying dead on the side of the road.

Traveler was lost. But 57 of his sons and daughters fought with the Confederates. More than 40 of them lived through the war. They passed on the Walking Horse gaits to the next generation.

## Grey John

Southern soldiers also kidnapped horses. Quite a few northern-bred horses stood in southern stables by the time the Civil War was over. Some of them got there the way a horse called Grey John did.

Grey John's mother was traveling through Tennessee with some Union soldiers when it was time for her **foal** to be born. She could not keep up, so the soldiers dropped her off at a farm. They took another horse and went on. That is how Grey John came to be born in a Tennessee barn. He was the **ancestor** of many modern Tennessee Walking Horses.

**Walking Horses are calm, obedient, and friendly.**

## Old Driver

Another northern horse was Old Driver. He came to Tennessee carrying a Union general on his back. The general rode up to the shop of Mike Earnheart, a Tennessee blacksmith. He asked Earnheart to take care of the exhausted stallion.

Earnheart nursed Old Driver back to health. Then he bred him with a Tennessee **mare**. Old Driver's grandson, Earnheart's Brooks, was one of the greatest Tennessee Walking Horses of all time.

**Tennessee Walking Horses give bounce-free rides.**

# Chapter 3

# Breeding the Walking Horse

The South struggled to rebuild after the Civil War. Everyone wanted horses for breeding. Tennessee Pacers and other gaited breeds were crossed with Thoroughbreds, Standardbreds, and Morgans. Some of their children lost the special gaits.

Tennessee breeders were determined to keep the Walking Horse gaits alive. They were very careful when crossing their Plantation Walking Horses and Tennessee Pacers with the northern stock. They made sure the foals would carry on the special gaits.

These breeders also tried hard to create a breed of horse with a good attitude. They tried not to breed horses that were mean or nervous.

**Tennessee Walking Horses get their qualities from many different breeds.**

They bred horses that were friendly and obedient. This effort increased the chances of getting foals that had the same attitude.

## The First Horse Show

Horse breeding became a major business in Tennessee after the Civil War. The two greatest stallions of that time were Grey John and Earnheart's Brooks. They both came from northern horses crossed with southern gaited horses.

Someone got the idea to stage a contest between the Grey John line and the Earnheart's Brooks line. This contest was something new. Horse shows were almost unheard of then.

The day was chosen. A huge crowd gathered at the Bedford County Fairgrounds. Grey John and Earnheart's Brooks were both there with dozens of their sons and daughters. All the horses that were old enough to ride were shown.

This early horse show was a huge success. But no one could agree on the winner. Some said Grey John and his children won the most honors.

**The people of Tennessee still take great pride in their special horses.**

Others said Earnheart's Brooks and his family were the winners.

Earnheart's Brooks did do a great trick at the show. He did a fast running walk in record time with his rider holding a glass of water on the palm of his hand. They did not spill a single drop.

## A Mixture of Horses

Tennessee Walking Horses get their qualities from many horses. Thoroughbreds give them strength and endurance. Saddlebreds give them a comfortable gait. Standardbreds give them a long

**Walking Horse shows are popular throughout North America.**

stride. Morgans give them a quiet spirit and gentle
manners. Just the right mixture of these horses produced
the Walking Horse.

During the 1880s and 1890s, Tennessee produced many
great Walking Horses. One was Black Allan, who was
born in 1886. His family tree was a mixture of breeds. It
included Standardbreds, Morgans, Thoroughbreds, and
Saddlebreds.

Black Allan could do the running walk. But more
importantly, he was able to pass this gait on to his
children.

Black Allan was bred with a good Walking Horse mare named Gertrude. The foal that was born was named Roan Allan. Roan Allan became the ancestor of many of today's top Walking Horses.

## Preserving the Tradition

The people of Tennessee took great pride in their special horses. Tennessee Walkers were intelligent and friendly. They were easy to work with and ride.

Anyone buying a Tennessee Walking Horse wanted to know its family tree. They were interested in knowing which famous old stallions were in its family. So breeders kept careful **pedigrees** of their horses.

Two Tennessee Walking Horse owners decided to start a breeding association. They invited all Walking Horse breeders to a meeting on April 27, 1935. This was the beginning of the Tennessee Walking Horse Breeders Association. Fifteen years later, in 1950, the Tennessee Walking Horse was recognized as an official

**Walking Horses come in every color a horse can be.**

breed by the United States Department of
Agriculture.

Walking Horse clubs soon started up across the
United States and Canada. Walking Horse shows
became big events. They drew competitors from
all over North America.

### Soring for Shows

Some trainers found a way to make their horses
step higher for the shows. They made their horses'
front legs or hooves sore. This practice was called

**soring**. Trainers would put on an **irritant**, or even burn or cut the leg or hoof. When the horse moved, the pain would make it lift its feet higher.

Some trainers were dishonest. They sored the feet of a horse of a different breed. The sored horse looked like it was doing a running walk. Then the trainer sold the horse. The buyers thought they were getting a Tennessee Walking Horse, but they were not.

Soring was cruel and dishonest. It was dangerous to the breed. Tricking buyers into thinking they had bought Walking Horses when they had not led to foals that did not have the Walking Horse gait. The breed will die out if too many horses lose the ability to perform the special gait.

The Tennessee Legislature made soring illegal in 1957. It is now against the law in most states and provinces.

Because the Tennessee Walking Horse has unique gaits that no other breed can perform, most Walking Horses are not bred with horses from other breeds. This practice has helped keep the Tennessee Walking Horse bloodlines strong.

# Chapter 4

# The Walking Horse Today

The Tennessee Walking Horses' unusual gaits are what set it apart from other breeds. When standing still, a Tennessee Walker looks similar to other all-purpose American breeds like the Morgan and **Quarter Horse**.

## What Tennessee Walkers Look Like

Walking Horses are of average height and build for a riding horse. A horse's height is measured from the **withers** to the ground. Most Walking Horses measure between 15 and 17 hands. A hand equals four inches (10 centimeters).

Tennessee Walking Horses weigh between 1,000 and 1,200 pounds (450 to 540 kilograms). They have a muscular build. Walking Horses take

**The three gaits of the Walking Horse are the flat-foot walk, the running walk, and the rocking-chair canter.**

very long steps. That is why they are able to perform such smooth gaits.

Tennessee Walking Horses come in every color a horse can be. Light-colored manes and tails are common. Many Walking Horses have white markings on their feet and faces.

## The Walking Horse Gaits

The Tennessee Walking Horse can place the back foot in front of the front foot without the two feet hitting against each other. This is called an **overstride**. The Walking Horse is the only breed that is able to perform it naturally. The three gaits of the Tennessee Walking Horse are the flat-foot walk, the running walk, and the rocking-chair canter.

## The Flat-foot Walk

The flat-foot walk is the slowest gait. It is actually a very fast walk compared to those of other horse breeds. Walking Horses travel about five miles (eight kilometers) per hour doing the flat-foot walk. The back foot hits the

**Walking Horses are as famous for their personalities as they are for their gaits.**

**Walking Horses are the horse of choice at many field trials.**

ground just ahead of the front footprint. The horse's timing is perfect. If it were not, the feet would hit against each other.

## The Running Walk

The running walk is similar to the flat-foot walk, but it is faster. Walking Horses travel at about 10 miles (16 kilometers) per hour doing the running walk. This is as fast as other horses trot. But the running walk does not have the bouncy, up-and-down motion of the trot.

Walking Horses have a funny habit when traveling at the running walk.

They often nod their heads to the beat of their feet. Some even swing their ears or click their teeth in perfect time.

## The Rocking-chair Canter

The rocking-chair canter is performed like the canter of other breeds. But the Tennessee Walking Horse's long stride makes its canter smooth and relaxed. The up-and-down motion of the Walking Horse's canter feels to the rider like sitting in a rocking chair.

## A Good Attitude

Tennessee Walking Horses are as famous for their personalities as they are for their gaits. More than a century of careful breeding has produced an entire breed of horses that is calm, obedient, and friendly. These traits make them favorites with families and people who cannot spend much time working with their horses.

Walking Horses also make good trail horses. Their calm attitude helps them meet the many challenges encountered in the wilderness.

# *Chapter 5*

# **The Walking Horse in Action**

Farmers and ranchers still use Tennessee Walking Horses in their fields. They are also favorites of park rangers who spend long days on horseback patrolling remote areas.

Walking Horses are a good choice for new riders and children. Their calm attitudes and bounce-free rides boost confidence for beginning riders.

## Walking Horses and Hunting Dogs

Tennessee Walking Horses are important to a North American sport called the field trial. It is a competition in which hunters on horseback use dogs to find birds. The Tennessee Walking

**The smooth Tennessee Walking Horse gaits are perfect for event riders.**

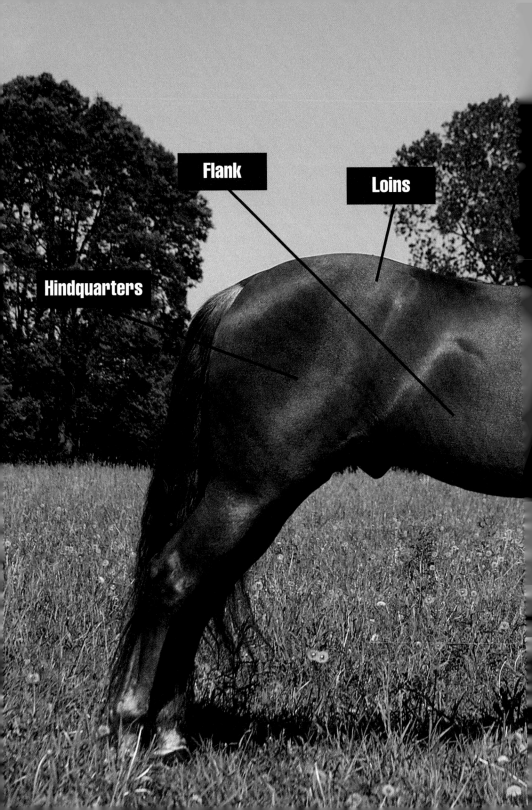

Horse is the horse of choice at many field trials.

Quail and pheasant are let out in a large field. Dogs search for them. The competitors ride horses and follow the dogs. The judges and spectators watch the event on their horses. Everyone is on horseback.

Any breed of horse can be used for field trials, but Tennessee Walking Horses are the most popular. Walking Horses have a quiet manner that lets the player pay attention to the dogs. The smooth gaits are perfect for riders spending all day in the saddle.

A Tennessee Walking Horse can be taught to stretch out when the rider mounts. This brings the horse's back down a little lower, making it easier for the rider to get on and off. Players must get off and on many times during the event.

**More than a quarter of a million Tennessee Walking Horses have been registered since 1935.**

## A National Celebration

Walking Horses compete in horse shows all over the United States and Canada. The biggest Walking Horse show is the Tennessee Walking Horse National Celebration. It is held every August in Shelbyville, Tennessee.

The National Celebration is the show every Walking Horse trainer hopes to enter at least once in a lifetime. It is the largest horse show in the United States. Thousands of people from all over North America come to watch the world's top Tennessee Walking Horses compete in a week of events.

## A Great Family Horse

More than a quarter of a million Tennessee Walking Horses have been registered since 1935. Only a small number are used for shows and sporting events. The majority of Tennessee Walking Horses are still doing what they were bred for more than a century ago. They are providing a great horseback-riding experience for everyone who rides them.

**Walking Horses can live from 20 to 30 years.**

# Glossary

**ancestor**—relative that comes before an individual animal or plant

**bay**—a reddish-brown horse with black legs, mane, and tail

**canter**—a slow running gait

**chestnut**—a reddish-brown horse

**colt**—a young male horse

**filly**—a young female horse

**flat-foot walk**—the slowest gait of the Tennessee Walking Horse, but actually a fast walk in which the horse places the back foot in front of the front hoof print

**foal**—a young horse

**gait**—the way a horse can move its feet to travel

**gaited horse**—a horse that can travel in special ways that other horses cannot

**gallop**—the fastest movement of a horse

**hand**—a unit of measurement equal to four inches (10 centimeters)

**irritant**—something that bothers

**mare**—a female horse

**Morgan**—a breed of horse that came from one famous stallion from Vermont

**overstride**—placing the back foot in front of the front footprint when traveling

**Quarter Horse**—a breed of horse first known for its speed in quarter-mile races, but now used as an all-purpose riding horse and workhorse

**pedigree**—a list of a horse's ancestors

**rocking-chair canter**—the especially smooth canter of the Tennessee Walking Horse

**roan**—a horse of any solid color with white hairs mixed in

**running walk**—the most famous gait of the Tennessee Walking Horse. The horse places the back foot in front of the front footprint when traveling as fast as or faster than other horses trot

**Saddlebred**—a breed of gaited horse native to the southern United States, known for its stylish looks

**soring**—the practice of irritating or hurting a horse's feet or legs so they will step higher for horse shows

**sorrel**—a reddish-brown horse with light-colored mane and tail

**stallion**—a male horse

**Standardbred**—a breed of horse used mostly for harness racing

**Thoroughbred**—a breed of racing horse that was bred in England

**trot**—a medium-fast step natural to all horses, easily recognized by its up-and-down action

**withers**—the top of a horse's shoulders

# To Learn More

**Edwards, Elwyn Hartley.** *Encyclopedia of the Horse.* New York: Dorling Kindersley, 1994.

**Green, Ben A.** *Biography of the Tennessee Walking Horse.* Nashville: Parthenon Press, 1960.

**Henry, Marguerite.** *Album of Horses.* New York: Rand McNally, 1951.

**Kainer, Robert A.** *The Coloring Atlas of Horse Anatomy.* Loveland, Colo.: Alpine Publications, 1994.

**Price, Steven.** *The Whole Horse Catalog.* New York: Brigadore Press, 1977.

You can read articles about Tennessee Walking Horses in the following magazines: *Discover Horses, Favorite Gait, Horse and Horseman, HorsePlay, Just About Horses, Voice of the Tennessee Walking Horse, Walking Horse Report,* and *Young Rider.*

# Useful Addresses

**American Horse Council**
1700 K Street NW, Suite 300
Washington, DC 20006-3805

**American Youth Horse Council**
4193 Iron Works Pike
Lexington, KY 40511-2742

**Tennessee Horse Council**
P.O. Box 69
College Grove, TN 37046-0069

**Tennessee Walking Horse Breeders' and
   Exhibitors' Association**
P.O. Box 286
Lewisburg, TN 37091-0286

**Walking Horse Trainers Association**
P.O. Box 61
Shelbyville, TN 37160-0061

# Index